Vi Khi Nao is such a wildly singula
her the last pen in my quiver and I
pants, our sweaty and shimmering

— Sawako Nakayasu, author of $

MW00698035

I give

, our

From

With formal experimentation and direct beckoning, Vi Khi Nao, draws us into this collection ripe with sound, sorrow, and sensuality. *A Bell Curve Is a Pregnant Straight Line* is a lyric calendar punctuated with playful wit and answers to questions you hadn't even thought to ask. The queer erotic is savored here—slurped like 'Sapphở.' Nao builds an anthropomorphized architure, and within it we find a certain uncanny order to things. 'But even intimate objects move.' In *A Bell Curve Is a Pregnant Straight Line*, Nao shows us that strangeness, amplified, can midwife new clarity and light up our dark mortal corners.

— **Alicia Mountain, author of** *High Ground Coward*

I believe in the ferocious, carnal and vegetal humanity of Vi Khi Nao's writing. Each new book adds to a quivering, entangled body of work and *A Bell Curve Is a Pregnant Straight Line* is my new favorite. It's grief-stunned, erotic, and wild. In Nao's lines, with their veering and encompassing ways, "no lover is solid" and yet the poet's gaze is "a potent, Sapphic one". The title poem took my breath away, and even describes the process by which that happened: "Her tears reach into my ribs / & pull out every single breath out of my chest". When you finish reading this blurb you should wash yourself in the coolness of its sobs: "anything that / Rhymes with the human pit." Incredible.

— **Jared Stanley, author of** *Book Made of Forest*

Vi's imagination oozes sex, buzzes with technology, gobbles food, and dances with goddesses, literary figures, a balloon artist, ancestors, and Sapphic ghosts. These poems grab me by the ovaries. I needed this corporeal poetry, poetry sloshing with fluids and brave bodies, at this very moment.

— **Kristy Lin Billuni, content creator of** *The Sexy Grammarian*

The inimitable genius of Vi Khi Nao is on full display in *A Bell Curve Is a Pregnant Straight Line*. Once immersed in her sensorium perception is heightened to the point of ecstatic convergence. The dramatic details are resplendent, volatile. Insight flashes like a searchlight. The poignancy of scintillation is "an iridescent hallucinogen" in dappled lines of brilliance. Interspersed throughout are Vi's enigmatic line drawings; the totality of this book is mesmerizing and astounding.

— **Brenda Iijima, author of** *Animate, Inanimate Aims*

Can poems be funny? I believe that Vi Khi Nao would say "yes!" I loved reading this work: it made me laugh, it made me want to write, it made me want to regard every single thing—the wood pile, a sweater, this table—as a thing alive and singing. Yes, singing because I don't know when, since listening to Mad Villain/MF Doom, I have encountered rhymes so delicious. Another striking thing about this collection is space. How delicately placed lacunae shape the page, making us really read each word and then savor the connections between: the joy of jumping the synapse. This savoring and active connection-making matters. "Matter" like "material" and "matrix" and "mother," Bracha Ettinger reminds us, which is the weaver's basis, the pre-modern grid where separate strands make a surface. And so this book is filled with webs and knots, crochet and cuts, shoulder pads and even skorts—a true hybrid. This is life as a big flexible bag of textile thought and utterance, a good shape for ease and difficulty, two textures that these poems and drawings make in the same time.

— **Jill Magi, author of** *Threads* **and** *Labor*

Imagine turning yourself—your whole body—inside-out, all the way, so that the you inside of you, i.e. every connected, reclusive, and/or unfathomable organ, cell, humor, sense, memory, affection and idea, became your new skin, profile and comportment. Then imagine looking and feeling, in that quasi-möbius and uncannily porous transposition, more like yourself than you ever felt before. Vi Khi Nao's *A Bell Curve Is a Pregnant Straight Line* is, for me, the transcendent, coruscating art of that sensation.

— **Brandon Shimoda, author of** *The Grave on the Wall*

A BELL CURVE IS A PREGNANT STRAIGHT LINE

KHI

VI

NAO

The author wishes to thank the following editors and friends:

Tania Sarfraz, Diane Williams, Prageeta Sharma, Brent Armendinger, Alicia Mountain, Steve Dickison, Kristy Lin Billuni, Coop Renner, Harilaos Stecopoulos, Major Jackson, Matt Hart, Tara Burke, Ana Paula, Rachel Levitsky, Emily Jungmin Yoon, Henry Finch, Karen Lepri, Kate McIntyre, Stephanie Anderson, Sheila Sumner, Casey McAlduff, Char McCutcheon, Kristina Marie Darling, Cheryl Clark Vermeulen, Dao Strom, Jennifer Ann Pilch Rita Mookerjee, Evan Isoline.

Requests for permission should be directed to 1111@1111press.com, or mailed to 11:11 Press LLC, 4732 13th Ave S, Minneapolis, MN 55407.

Cover Art "Uterus Love" Copyright © 2021 by Sophia Trinh

Paperback: 978-1-948687-40-9

Printed in the United States of America

FIRST AMERICAN EDITION

9 8 7 6 5 4 3 2 1

A
BELL
CURVE IS
A PREGNANT
STRAIGHT LINE

for GIOVAN

POETIC
Shorts, Shirts, Skorts, Skirts

A tragic first date. An evicted fetus. A restaurant called Sapphò. The flu. Argiope spiders. A room. The sea. Body parts as clothing. A long poem. A short one. A long one. Flipping like Morse signals, the poems in this collection gather under the pregnant arc of the bell curve in four quadrants that gestate desire. They scatter and sprawl across the page, or shrink in demure bundles, become pen-and-ink drawings, become lists, perform a termite insurrection against style.

The author gratefully acknowledges the following publications in which poems in *A BELL CURVE IS A PREGNANT STRAIGHT LINE* first appeared, sometimes in slightly different form:

"Using Walnut As Cloth." *Elimae*, Fall 2009

"The Tenant." *NOON*, Spring 2012

"The Phone Booth." *VISIONS*, Spring 2012

"Liquid Mucus." & "Shoulder Pads." *The Iowa Review*, Fall 2013

"The Room In Five Moods of Cannots." *Ploughshares*, Spring 2013

"Urine Inmates." *Forklift, Ohio*, Fall 2015

"Lady Gaga Apples." *The Lesbian Body*, Fall 2017

"A Bell Curve Is A Pregnant Straight Line." *Belladonna**, Spring 2017

"The Definition of Charisma & Resent." *Crevice*, Summer 2017

"Nautical Shrouds." *Asian American Writers' Workshop*, Winter 2017

"The Room: An Anthromorphized Collection." *Projective Industries*, Spring 2018

"Homeless Possibilities." *SpeCt books*, Spring 2019

"The Afternoon On Impulse" & "Good Marriages Should Live On Ice." *The Best American Poetry Blog*, Spring 2019

"Widow." *Pangyrus*, Spring 2020

"Sapphǝ." *diaCRITICS*, Fall 2020

"Being A Square Is Not Enough." *La Vague Journal*, Fall 2020

"Video of Your Pre-Lunch Tour." *La Vague Journal*, Fall 2020

"Algorithm Forever." *Split Lip Magazine*, Spring 2021

"Cashews." *Selffuck*, Spring 2021

CONTENTS

SHORTS

SAPPHở

I   h u s h   the etymology of your fingers

By tasting the eternal night   around their   tips

Fennel   immolates   your desire into my broth

I am   clavicle   not vulture   cleaving your aniseed for pain

I h u s h the wilderness   near your basin-shaped   cavalcade

You elevate   in your throes of ardor &   I bend to meet

Your feminine furniture   legs   and all   as a reference

For   diptyque & civility   If your tongue is one type of

Transitive verb   Will my lips be   able to take

Yours as a direct object for   a complication of time?

My left cheek seeks in sequence   the grammar of your breath

The translucent material   of your fugaciousness

As   you lean   from syntax into chopstick

If time identifies herself as a pansexual & you agree to be the nodes on my laptop

If my desire is binary + yours has urinary tract infection

Won't it be cruel   if I suggest   we all sleep together,

Muscle & all,   on a bed of salt & oysters?

Won't it be fun   for bivalves to be bisexual ?

To open a Vietnamese restaurant for lesbians called Sapphở?

WIDOW

God,

You carry this device in my chest called   *love*

& I - a child of infertility - choose you to sterilize

the left *testicle* of intimacy   While sitting on the right

(*hand, of course*) I grope the goose which is your *ghost*

Not holy not resurrection not an assault on the Nature

of Divinity :::: *God,* you once castrated my belief in you

It *was February* or *March* in a sublet in Brooklyn

& I (still) respond by *emasculating* your vision of toilet paper

Hand sanitizer   hands clapping into a Berlin night

Let me be clear :   the door is not *you,* the skylight isn't me gazing

down at *you,* the window isn't your *widow*

I never view you as anybody's *hard husband*   *Never* wed *for* now

Let me *be empty* - the Indo-European root signifier for *widow*

Let me *bereft*

Let me *leave* your bed side while I *neuter* you out of my own private *galaxy*

A PORTRAIT OF A LADY ON FIRE[1]

If the gaze, a potent sapphic one, could detox anyone

Give the visual asshole a natural colon cleanse

It would be that *gaze* that Héloïse bestows upon Marianne

On that quarantine island in Brittany

I didn't care for the nonchalant abortion with

The children acting as make-shift pots and pans

I didn't care for the *O rph e us* reference, which seems silly in the modern era

Who would want a memory when anyone could have the actual thing ?

Nor the random ghastly appearance of the wedding dress

I will confess though a painting has every right not

To be a painting

I will confess that my hands did grow tired watching Hélène Delmaire, the

True artist behind the scene (her real hand the *factual faint s m o k e*)

Sketch and limn, *thick swatch of paint*, her optical signature, could behave like a

Blindfold as if to erase our eyesight through another lens of seeing

Perhaps I want *love* to be that hungry gale

That *hypothermic brisk* that island so capable of *torturing the hairs*

Of Sciamma's sharp protagonists

How does it feel to film a former lover ?

To see her act carnally with another ? Perhaps for this sole reason

The bedroom passion was distinctly *smothered & curated* by

Women being tossed into an island already ablaze with canvas

---

[1] *for Alyse*

Soaked in *sea water*   soaked on page 28 of an *iridescent* , hallucinogen

Armpit of a drug   the true *auxiliary*   bushy remedy for a *clitoris*

I did care   how could I not?   for the music the eyes

Could make   taking me a *fervent hostage* in its brief soliloquy of *queer rage*

ALGORITHM FOREVER

My body is April

Modified for your March hips daffodil sprawl

As sporadic as the way you withdrew your lungs from the bronchial purse of June

I am May. Totally on display

For your infinite computation of rainwater

Saturating that August robustness

Drunk on a full cup of Leo

We agree that February is incompetent

Totally socially dependent on January and March for guidance as to where to land
    the snow

Widen your hips please

July is walking through in her bikini stroll

Half the year

I am inside you

Half the world around the convenient store of your calendar moon

I watch September and November menstruate

Watch the numbers march in and out

Wearing wet boots made of hemoglobin

Wearing shoelaces made of iron

Waiting for the mini snow pads with wings that December provides with hypothermic
    want

I know you have the coronavirus

You are as logarithmic as you are lethargic

Even when I make you grate ginger over hot water in our Google Doc

Ask you to stash a bowl of rice in your wallet

And tease you about the drone view of my buns

When this pandemic is over

I am opening two pomegranates

Near my breasts for you

CASHEWS

I was sleeping so deeply   until *three* bags

Of cashews, pumpkin seeds, and almonds   all climbed up on

My bed to sneeze & crack up these unbalanced,

Nutty, *psychotic jokes* on the nature of same sex

Video-taping & same sex *lubricants* - carnal butter to massage onto

The bony *asses* of   cashews

I prefer the generic name   for   *tree climbing* in same sex marriage

I prefer   the prefix   for   13 grams of salt

I could lick   anything   off that hemp   flower which you idolize

Which you call   your own rich resource of protein

Love me   processed   *love* me with just enough *anacardic acids*

Love me   until I see our personal *dermatologist* for my rash

In one video your lips were so full

Take   my glass of water from our *nightstand*

& *empty* it out   to   make room for your *saliva*

For your   sweet mouth which abducts

My *geraniums* in the middle of the night

I am saturated in *ether*

I *long* to breathe   while holding an aquarium near you

I *long* for the three girls to tie their *plastic hair* together

To *sit* quiescently on the edge of a *lake*

To *wait* for them to fall over

To *listen* while they *drown*

BEING A SQUARE IS NOT ENOUGH

You are a *helium balloon* episode she tells me

& you need a square

Have I told her I am drawn to *rhombicosidodecahedron* ?

She has 120 edges   No lover is solid

No human can have that many faces

Until I collided with her

In another video   I am a frozen vegan cake

In which she keeps eating and eating me

Until what is left   of me   is no longer savory

I am just *a debris* of softness ,   flour   ,   shortening

Widening   my *Scandinavian* origin for more sugar crumbs

There is an alternative route to rolling me

Over   like flat bread   There is this thing called *humility*

Which can stop the *bakery* of my poor sexual appetite

From *inflating*   I tell her: your vegan diet can't just be me

I am *leavening*   I *levitate*   I   do *yoga* for 48   hours in the oven

I love you in *chicken oil,* in *duck fat,* in *zucchini rhombus*

I wait for her to take a nap   Then I open another video

Of   me being cut into a *pizza* slice   with   *eight edges*

This is where I am no   longer   vegan

Because   there is   a   long   thick   blanket

Of   Torta   del Casar   DOP   Virgen del Prado   cheese

Made of   raw sheep's milk   lying on top of me

Love is complicated   because there is *no nobility*

In being a noble gas   There is   *no thermonuclear fusion*

In eating somebody today &   the next day not

There is only one *airship* in my heart &

It has *three bullet holes* already in it

VIDEO OF YOUR PRE-LUNCH TOUR

Your unwashed hair is no monsoon
As I stroke like a dust pan to sweep light into your mouth
I always think there is something militant
About not being able to touch you across the room
From America - from what strength will your lipstick make available
Which I intangibly can't take forward
Tonight we each take turns teaching each other
How to nail the coffin into an idea
How to connect mother destiny with a sea of karmic particles
How to lower my torso for the angle which could be your gaze
or hip   or calisthenic strips
Had I seen you take that ghat ? To give your eyes that much deserved bath
of imperial expansion   such orange and gold horizon
Which matches all your hair across the four quadrants of my desire
My face does not mismatch   an empty door for freewill
Won't confuse you waking up in the morning for a spoon of olive oil
How terrible is my tea kettle ?
For refusing to take a reflection as a sign of genuflection
For giving your thighs a small detour of my lower torso
Take your full breasts into my hands
And watch my tongue wave hello to
your earlobe like a repossessed handkerchief
from the fragile mouth of a townhouse

TOTE BAG

My love,

You are committed to me like a marriage

And, I reason, before crest & apogee

With intimate extreme has seen your armpit

Hair   before kissing the supreme leader

Inside of your female body which I call

A tall glass of lucent water

Tonight   the summer gives me a lucid bath

Where the photograph you've taken of me

Without any maximum speed   has not developed

Itself on your hostel's ceiling like a cauliflower

Being broken apart on a basin made of

Ligature of fear.   Flowers,   you have the foresight

to say: immortality is a

bath I can't give you   after you return from a

war with a patrician of emptiness

The tote bag of the subconsciousness that you

carry with you over your shoulder

is still a tote bag   Am I wrong to want all of you

The way an Aristocratic family in Ancient Rome

Wants the head of the dead ?

After waiting to kiss you   I become supple

Not superlative   not flawless   not marvelous

I walk softly into your videos   while you lie

Unimpressed like a   statue

I am herbal and muscular ready to sedate

Your gaze with a nipple piercing I gave to both

The Hippocampus & the Heraclitus inside

The wholesome chamber of my isolated self

Won't you place your tongue there

So I know the difference between a moan & water?

HOMELESS POSSIBILITIES

-mischievous lungs

-indented desires

-broken fornication

-relative vagina

-knee warmers

-cheesy hardware stores

-boring pimple pushers

-terrified juicer

-contentless spatula

-exorbitant microwave

-infrequent euphoria

-unaware toilet paper

-sweaty vacuum cleaner

-cardiovascular rest stop

-commanding armpits

LIQUID MUCUS

My nose   has   been   away
& is afraid to come home

                    To my face

My face   has   been   berating
The bridge
       Build   a better one
That allows a birch   log
             Of   a finger
To cross it

                  During a flood

The cold came &

               It has been raining

The sentries
      Come in the form of liquid

Mucus &
Barricade the pair
Of lungs—

                 Floating gutters

SHOULDER PADS

my aorta   hangs

in the closet of my body   like a sports jacket

it   doesn't get windy here   but the sleeves are   shaking

falling in love   with you has made me   feel

as if my   heart has been sewn   with shoulder pads

perhaps   to give my shaggy left & right ventricles   a more robust appeal

uplifting   frame of emotional

&

sexual squareness

shoulder pads are no longer popular   any more

you wonder if my heart has receded to the 1980s

you gaze down at my sock drawer:

only the kidneys & lungs are paired

everything else, it seems, is missing a sock

you wonder why sometimes one foot

is dipped in spleen   &   the other in gall bladder

you are just like me you know   this

interlockingcloset thing

unb uttoning   my heart   one blood vessel   at a time as my heart   slides   into your jacket

                    shoulder pads over shoulder pads

i dangle in your closet space

while pulling   (into twilight)   one errant thread   floating

          on the surface of   your aorta

URINE INMATES

your argiope spider is

peeing a thread of white

light

it's hard to be outdoors

& not use its

conveniently web-based

latrine

meanwhile the sun

thinks: I want to donate

my subconscious

to your handmade

vertical hammock: will

your gods – verdant

photosynthetic

consumers – be willing

to absorb such blatant

acts of banana

generosity?

sure, responds the

banana spider politely

on behalf of the leaves.

NO! reply the leaves.
you will melt the smallest
outdoor prison in the
world. go away. we are
urine inmates. leave us
in the dark!

CROCHETING

his penis is a yarn

crocheting the sweater of my flesh
once in a while
the sweater dreams of floating
on the balcony getting dried from the heat

when   the rain   comes   pouring   down, heaving
stitching   the eye of rain
through my carnal blanket   my breasts would pretend to be
            two balls of short stories

                                        dropping down the cliff
the mattress

what now

what now

crocheting   crocheting

when my sweater comesundone   from   the

                                                    his tongue

a birthday candle   extinguishing

as the wax drips

                                        becomes a blind girl

USING WALNUT AS CLOTH

He is pushing the log up into the house while

the house keeps on collapsing, wanting

to overflow the riverbed. Monthly.

His piece of log is finally occluded.

What must he do when the dismantled house is

falling

falling

      a   part

& he wants to push*his*log up the hill.

What will happen?

Goat cheese, organic dates, yellow apple.

THE PHONE BOOTH

He wires his heart to the base

of my spine. In his heart lies a red door with green vines.

I say, this is divine.

I say this with my heart on the floor, my toenails pointed to the stars,

& the rivers of many dark worlds revolving through the skull of time.

His breath tastes like night or numbers printed on a knob.

His arms, riddled by ancient scribes, enclose me like a box

on a sea of dust.

I am told

I am a lily that

he folds & unfolds.

I am pressed against his chest—

Leaves hung & strapped to the subliminal walls of paper & books.

He unwraps me in his sleep

like a snake shedding its skin.

Dreams crawl on their belly, make their way through daylight by sweating out of

my skin.

Sometimes like the lily spouting out of the mountain,

I am alone here.

Fumbling through the dark while he tucks my body away from the wind.

After this,

his touches

in the dark

are like volcanoes

erupting

before the window: the sun gleams.

I am tied to his body

like a knot.

The heat from his body.

The sweat from his skin.

How do I unknot

this tie

& have his heart

ride through my spine

like

a phone book

chained to a phone booth?

LADY GAGA APPLES

I am elated

I have been

Supinated near a hyphenated

Teabag-whale who introduced me to

A geoponic door

Beneath

The ocean floor

Where

I heard a hydroponic-potential seahorse

Qhispered to an electroreceptive fish

That muay thai or tai chi was a type of spicy Thai dish

+ that he should try it with electrocuted cockroaches

I feel my untouched

Egg sacs lower their

Libido-shy libido

I think life is too short

To use raw onion as nipple rings

On my cetacean body

My nipples are tucked away

Like wheels

On an airplane during take offs

When my body revokes

The retractable nipples from

The aquatic air

My fragile concentric jewelry

Get crushed in the process

Damaging my

Precious collection of

Perishable gems

THE AFTERNOON

Just before morning closes

Your hands dismiss

Razored on the edge

Couldn't resonate with me

ON IMPULSE

Her deformed smile

Respiratory foams

Your face

So let us be foes in the aftershave

GOOD MARRIAGES SHOULD LIVE ON ICE

Slender glacier teases the innocent husband

To hand over his wife, the ice tray.

The icy husband resists

Of course, he resists

The wife, divided & compartmentalized

Sometimes the husband notices a pool by his side

Love is confusing: indeed, when husband can't gather wife together

On Sunday & on thirsty days

Husband places three quarters of wife in a glass

No one believes in singing with divided tears

A choir is required, & then a drink to quench the thirst of voices

Husband can't believe that wife

Can hold a mosquito that long

He can brush away her subconscious

By draining her of her liquid free will

Sometimes volition doesn't belong to husband entirely

Sometimes wife can be thick, like jello

Even solid objects can be unfaithful.

THE SLEEPING BAG OF INSOMNIA

Sleeping on the floor is like being in jail- Jim Weaver

Embedded in the regime

Of beauty

Your imagination unleashes

Its currency of

Sleeping on the floor

Of time

The verb "   " gets on its knees

To pontificate before climbing into

The sleeping bag of insomnia

Climb out

      Climb in

           The hole

Sometimes you have to betray

In order to be faithful

The verb "to suck" hasn't

Been given an opportunity

To give a blowjob yet

So it spends its remaining days

Being a "sucked up."

SHIRTS

A BELL CURVE IS A PREGNANT STRAIGHT LINE

What does coolness look like?

A block of ice/

The size of an entire estate in Moscow?

A cubic foot of cloud?

With corners touching & sensing its own borders like a nebulous blind sitting in

an invisible cage made of atmosphere/

What if I were to pull you into my arms ?

Would you drop into a bullet

Because you feel the weight

Of it?   You r   toes.

Or would you float beneath the awning of my armpit

Because the lightness of my awning   held your non-aromatic nostril

Together like a door knob/

Perhaps you feel the weight of my kiss merely because

You are in my arms sliding up &

Down like a teardrop that has climaxed to the tip of your

Forehead hair.

When I held you in

My arms   I felt the levity of lead   & the density

Of your tears

After all, you had been crying &
When I held you   pulled you not like a thread to tooth
But like a forklift to snow

When I held you in my arms   you arched your body backward   just a little –
Or maybe
You are light like a summer equinox

When your tears fall on my blouse   your sea sits like a stone on the throne
Of the human river.
You are at home
Painting over Cézanne.

In my arms, you are mistaken.

Your teardrop, I mean. Or was it your window of opportunity?

Which was maybe a mistake
Because my armpit isn't a cockpit
Crying is not an act of flight. For cats. For chimpanzees/
Or is it?
When you begin to cry - you are descending toward a mountain
In your solar plane of solitude.

Confusing. Anticipation – for

A Kleenex box.

You pull on my sleeve & you sob

Just a little into it.

Later when your wrist is aware of itself—

It feels a pool of gourmet

Nasal output

Definitely

Definitely

Made of mucus, 2 hours of sobbing

Sitting wet on my sleeve—

I think

I learned to elbow chicken thighs by submitting to chicken thighs. You asked
your mother if you could color her underwear with the melancholy of tomorrow while your friends chill out with diaper rash. Sometimes your mother borrows underwear from your grandfather & your grandfather lays on
the sofa naked like a tub of vanilla ice cream with his antiqued snicker bar
from mid-30s pointing at your new Apple computer. People begin to smile
a certain way because your aunt hasn't fucked the kitchen sink yet. Not yet.
The phone keeps on ringing while your niece cries into a remote control, in
which case her wailing changes channels and you begin to acquire an aftertaste
for Spanish soap opera. Somewhere your uncle climbs into his pickup truck
and fucks the cigarette holder because he couldn't finger-fuck the water bottle
while your aunt was staring at the cap. And before your face embarrasses the
station wagon, the back of your pants frown at the chairs. No one can discern
the difference between creases and frowns. And as luck has it, you remove your

symmetry of garnish. You tease the moon left and right with your perversity of seawater. No luck will carry your wind-chill vipers like a pack of wolves trying to backtalk a cow in French. You stare out into the landscape for some instrument of morbidity. The landscape loses sexual interest in fertile land and your verdant gaze on eggplants can't change the colors or the desire of the pan that holds everything sweet and salty with its teeth. September renews her membership on your skin and you unlock yourself a little just so that your niece can grow some chest hair and baby talk to you in a low submissive voice in Russian. In Russia there is a diffusion of silence. In which case you took the wrong exit out of tempura. You knew its branches were crunchy and Japanese and you had wanted to marry the sushi stall with your French fries and burger. No one murders anyone, but blood doesn't know the language of a knife or bullet or car accidents on a free freeway of highways. You knew your brothers would hijack your aunt's assembly line of tongues with their brutish lips and their mustaches laddering a storm of saliva. You knew breakfast had been prepared for the journey and you smiled backward into an envelope.

Sorry I digress some

What I mean to say

Is that it is not okay in winter

To cry on my sleeve. Summer is okay.

& Maybe Spring

Because when that pool of mucus turns itself

Into one slab of ice

My bloodstream from

That regional sleeve

Stops moving to my fingertips

When my blood stops moving itself

Around in that area

It means that my hand

From that glacial sleeve

Won't function any more

So to undo your bra I have to exert several Newtonian laws

It feels like a million tons or

What my head feels like

Or empty

Like a gun without any bullets.

Maybe I should be

Clear to you my audience – why my beloved

Had been crying   – on our first date

That day she learned that she had breast cancer

At the age of ¼ of a century   or better put a perfect cube

Because I am black, tall, thin, & European

Ready to fuck anything

Supreme + cancerous –

At least that's what my OKCupid

Profile declared when she met up with me

That block   of exquisite human ice

In feminine form

& cancerous/

My OkCupid Is NOT OK.

When I said cancerous

I meant   the astrological sign – like

Scorpio or Pisces or Taurus

Not actually cancer itself.

I had wanted to unclasp her bra

To face the two dying

Birds   that sat on the

Fabric railing of her chest

Throughout dinner— I had no idea

They were sitting on the edge of that railing

50 stories high on that skin of hers

thinking about jumping   planning her final suicide

Does it take cancer to make a date meaningful?

Maybe this is what it is like to be submissive

Before two dying, winged, bipedal, endothermic, egg-laying knockers

Dressed in banana leaf bras

When I gaze at her breasts

I think of the twin towers

When the first came down, I imagined

This is the future

I knew in this quasi-Arabian night

That it was an accident

This thing that came to her deformed

I knew Cancer was a terrorist attack on the

Mammary gland

I have known – in this state of shock – as I was

Holding her

What is terrorism

But an imbalance of soot & ash

& fallen cement/stone?

Why do you have bras made of banana leaves in the middle of Denver, Colorado? I ask her.

She replies that banana leaves are great placemats for her breasts. & she says that Google said that banana leaves are large, flexible, & waterproof.

& I think of the both of us   as I hold her hand

I think dates like this   I do not feel like a black queen

Standing next to her pearly white queenness, a queen as well

As she proceeds to checkmate me

With her dying, cancerous gaze

I am in the corner with my

Lonely ice & my lonely

Stone of a heart

My king is eating breakfast without me

Dying as we speak

This ruin

This teardrop on soot

Creating a hole in the atmosphere

The window in which forms

This tenderness

I am on my

Knees

My tongue reaching to confirm the darkness of her skin

Beautiful, hypnotic, enchanting

As my tongue licks

The tips of her nipples

As if my tongue were a lighter

Lighting two candles made of

Human milk & desire

When the wicks, pink like cherry,

Stand up straight burning

Like eternal votive –

I know terrorism

Doesn't wear a brassier   - which is a fancy

Way of saying— to blow things up

& Out of proportion   — to bow down

low to training bras   — which is

radiation

which means to take off one's bras   is to take off Boeing 767-200ER —

I pull her into my arms & she sobs into them as if

I were a cave

I pull her into the symmetrical ruin, the home of my heart —

In which —

There were these warning signs

These alarm bells

When she wore that shirt   — I swore

Something was wrong — when I unbuttoned each

Her bra made of banana leaves stitched together by blue synthetic

Thread — the clasp

I told her

Your female form is a jungle —

As her banana leaves fell on the edge

Of that memory foam before rolling their angulated cups onto themselves so that

They looked like two nodes of headphones, containers of tropical mammary music,

Were getting to know their concave selves better

If you must face an echo while you are an echo - why not

Be a symposium for

Two cancerous pearly introverts?

Why not let Plato play around with her female Play-Doh

With rhetorical knockers, logical tits, mathematical mamillas.

If an echo had to find its soulmate

In a concaved proscenium — such as the cup of a brassier — why not let Beethoven's Symphony #5 be the crescendic altitude of a kiss

As I kiss every centimeter of her

Skin while she sobs into me —

My armpit, my cockpit, my spit, — anything that

Rhymes with the human 'pit'

The tits are exposed to light

The cups of the bras

Are turning their twin

Concaved satellites

The cups of the bras

Even if they were to fold their cups together

As if to clap

For the hidden symphony

Of the heart

The valve - a trombone

Blowing the blood vessels into euphoria

Of lemon + cadence

When I pull her into my arms

My body blows out all her candles

In the darkness my skin is spray-painted

With the white, wet soot of her

Breasts' expiration dates — the expiration dates of some indefinite future

Between the yearning to hold & the craving to

Desire

Before I can say anything comforting

Her tears reach into my ribs —

& pull out every single breath out of my chest

Like pulling an innocent child out of hiding

In that closet

Made only for

Trembling bone marrow

In my arms

Her eyelids grow heavy — when her eyelashes comb

The crooked floor of my neck

Something tells me

This is how a gravel road

Is formed

For

Modern trafficking & training ground

In preparation for the exploitation

Of one single landscape

Where do I want her now — as I turn to a kettle to make her a cup of tea – now that she has stopped sobbing & ¼ of a century is sprawled out on my bed sheets & that ¼ of a century has fallen asleep on my bed sheets   A sob is the voice of a teacup   which has lost its handle

Even when hot   — at boiling point — the cup wants to be held –   not to get warm or warmer   but to possess the opportunity to cool down

SKORTS

THE   TENANT

She is a tenant who lives approximately three feet above moving ground, in an apartment complex that generally holds one tenant at a time. In a couple of months, she will be forced to evacuate. Until then, when she sleeps, she presses her face against the spine of the room. But during these darkest months, she is bald & thrives like an old man on life support, with food feeding through the tube. It must be a drag to have a cord sticking through her center like a VCR. Sleeping near the spine is like her being inside the grapevine.

They ship her to the morgue. I hop from one apartment complex to another, but the first one is always my favorite. It's like being on a trampoline. From my thin walls, I hear two neighbors shouting. My landlord & a man. This happens quite often. Like being near the idiot box when Cops is on. I like the first landlord most. She communicates by pressing her hands on her wall or my abode. Sometimes she gets to know me by bearing large gifts.

I am now ten at another landlord's. I am trying to reattach myself to the VCR by placing the white cord around the top of the bunk bed post. From there I will hang down. I remember the early days. Surrounded by walls. The sounds of the fluid moving through my skull. What river has gotten me into space & left me dangling?

NAUTICAL SHROUDS

I have spent my life roaming deliberately. Exhaling oxygen out of triangular shaped ventilators. I turn to the coral reefs & have measured my life by their verdant glances. Their lungs, by the way, are fake corridors. & although I wag my tail, I am not a dog chained to a leash. Nor do I need the approval of my peers. I roam. Sometimes in solitude; sometimes in a crowd. But unlike a dog, I do not die a little each day, subdued to the loyalty of my master. I die all at once if it must be. I die sometimes wrapped up in the sleep of nautical shrouds. Sometimes alone with a bow needle nailed to the roof of my mouth. Sometimes my jaw is completely yanked out of my body & this is okay. This gives my body an opportunity to watch my decapitated head fall into an ice bucket. This time I really kick the bucket — my cousin's face pressed against my mandibles as our fleshes are taken from us. I do not expect my last breath to exist at the corridor of another face.

THE ROOM IN FIVE MOODS OF CANNOTS

The room cannot feel its arteries stuffed with animal fat from the insulation. Cannot hope to alter its mouth & eating is not a thing that it can do well. The room hasn't taken a bath since 1987, but there was a slight wash in 1992 that bestowed on the room its perforated body. The room cannot control the content of its character. Cannot control if happiness is a regular visitor of the closet. What can it control? The room can sit naked for a really long time until someone moves in. Sometimes at night, the room falls in love with the refrigerator near the sink. Cannot help but stare at the light & the carton of eggs & the miniskirts of green onions & the underpants of cilantro floating on the clothes hangers of the cilantric stem. The room doesn't want to be redundant, but how can it write a love letter to something that cannot even cross its legs?

THE DEFINITION OF

CHARISMA: A personality disorder involving the use of magnetism to generate social order 2) the ability to gather light from others & make it emanate from one's eyes & mouth & face 3) in context of a leader, a charismatic individual gains economic & social advantages by smiling widely & destroying others or the lives of others in the process. Sometimes smiling widely & exuding magnetism encourage the activities of artifice 4) it is related to the cousin of charm, but charisma can carry ominous flair & become more charming in its sadistic methods 5) an establishment of attractiveness & civilizational appeals.

RESENT: A verb at best, a thing maybe, a profession. Depending on the circumstances, it can be a brief or extensive career with acidity not related to melons, limes, lemons, grapefruits, green apples, etc. MEANINGS: The ability to deliver an invested emotion back into a certain location of the body, such as on the tip of the hypaxial muscles or along the ribcage of the chest. RESENT has the following siblings: RESENTS, RESENTED, RESENTMENT, RESENTER(S), & other members who neglect to appear on this page. RESENTMENT has an infrequent birthday & will only celebrate the anniversary of its birth if it remembers. This explains why large celebrations are usually followed by infrequent smaller ones. Resentment, for instance, is not like fish or lettuce when it enters the body of its host. It's more like beef. When the host ingests it, the parasite sits & rots & never really truly goes away. RESENTMENT, as a profession, has a teaching assistant named ANGER, which feeds its stomach with more educated parasites. These intellectual parasites live for days & months & years before being subdued by other primitive parasites such screaming & fisting. Sometimes RESENTMENT retires to a place of comfort before climbing a hill to disappear into the wilderness of other emotion-related creatures. RESENTMENT descended from the French in 1610. After that, like the invention of the icemaker, everyone had to have it.

SKIRTS

THE ROOM:
an anthropomorphized meditation

The room is aware of the heartbeats stepping on the stones of the
stairs. The mouth
returns to the
doorknob. Wounded by
the door, the mouth
refuses to sip ginger
ale. At the end of the
pasta

deconstruction, the mouth takes another bite of the red tomato.
The room stares
helplessly — the
mastication ritual of
the mouth. The room
thinks of Rie Hosokai.
Of her mouth before
the creation of the
inflatable pump. Her
mouth is exercising
air precaution. & for
this, she is rewarded
with the lust of

design. The mouth feeds
itself with deluded

red sauce & the spaghetti noodles descend the esophagus. Ropes
dangling off the cliff,
waiting to receive the
pool of the diaphragm.
Chasm & quiet dolor.
The room can't shake
the dust that blows
through its screen.
The rain falls down
to clean, to shake the atmosphere of the afternoon.

The room is willing to take Bus 60 into the sea. The sun is
willing. The fingers
trace the contours of
the skyline while the
pigeons peck on the
chest of the financial
district. Hangnails
leave a trail of
goosebumps down the
room's back. The street
cannot reimburse
itself with traffic
fare. A woman bids
another man farewell
at the bus depot.
Hangnail is killing

the room's sense of
mute trepidation. The
bus arrives in a blur.
Four women debate the
social   orientation
of   the   bus.   What
number   amongst   the
civilization of buses.
The   woman   descends
into the tent called
Black Pearl. The light
of   the   sea   shakes
the   current.   Water
breathes out silk &
stops dreaming about
being human.

In September, the room closes its door & opens its window to
the coming of pastoral
November.   The
bourgeois of June &
July, the months of the
middle class, rarely
come to revolutionize
the calendar, to make
all the months of the
year   socialist.   The
trust fund babies, the
Benjamins, the upper
class of January &
February & perhaps
March   regain   their
regal, affluent stance
on the amphitheater of

the weeks. The thongs
of days shout & beat
their fists against
their chest, demanding
their work days to
lengthen & shorten at
different times. The
upper middle class of
April & May refrain
from getting involved

with the sweat glands of their incoming neighbors. They walk
along the shoreline
of rain, daffodils, &
cherry blossoms. They
confide in themselves
& feign compatibility
with the upper class,
whose wrath involved
subzero terrains &
snow banks that wilt
away their blooming
morning glories,
roses, lilies, Spring
flowers. Sometimes the
upper middle class
hides their animosity
by

bringing soft, gentle breeze from the North. Sometimes bearing
quiet gifts of warmth
& silly lilies of the
valley. But lately
they, the Benjamins,

have been known for
their sheepskin & wolf
mandibles. The birds
are most gullible.
They return from
their winter houses in
Florida. Their wings
chip off in midflight.
From a distance they
look like bullets that
have lost

their explosive insights. Near the bottom of the totem pole, the
semi-mendicants, or
indigents of the
calendar year. Their
lives are over even
before they begin to
enlist their children
of their days for free
lunches at St. Mary's.
They fill their empty
stomachs with candies
from the witch. They
grow weary from
converting hot air
into cold air. Their
engines are overworked
& they slave away for
basically nothing. They
sit on street corners
wondering how do they
break their cycle of
enslavement. They chew

on their fingers & pray
despite the fact that
their toenails are
growing longer. The
lowest class of the
year shivers in the
thin blanket of ice.
Even Akhmatova threw
her poems into her
oven & had to rewrite
them from memory.
Sometimes time is a
fascist. Sometimes
a francophile. A
communist.

The clouds remember the sun rising in their mouth. The sun
returns to kiss the
dust. The clouds lower
their torsos to the
ground, inhaling the
snowballs of dust as
they tumble into the
sun. Noise & firefly
& heartbeat. Winter
descends the long hill
of Fall to collapse on
the familiar unpaved
road of snow. Mouth
sinks into the bottom.

Winter winter eats
eats eats the membrane
of Spring. The clouds
hover above the room.
The clouds haven't
bent over for anyone.
How do they know how
to brush the dust off
their knees? How aware
are they that they are
slaves to the earth?
After a girl with
flowers on her shoes
climbs into the bus,
the lips of the wallet
open wide. On the bus,
the air is up. Up
like yuppies before
adopting a child.
The room worries that
the clouds will hover
over the toilet bowl.
The fog has entered
the halls of sadness.
Clouds & fog compare
the colors of their
skin with one another.
On the street, a man
in a blue shirt holds a
woman's hand. From his
facial expression, he
is afraid that she will
outlive him. The left
side of his eyebrow

lifts higher. It is a strong indication that his preoccupation with age & death has accelerated four fold. To counter his vexation & to relieve him of the envy of outliving, he releases her hand & pushes her out into the street away from the sidewalk. Her face twists slightly to express her surprise. A feeling of betrayal enters her face & the elation on her face minutes earlier when he was holding her hand disappears. She is sad now. Three weeks ago, her face turned blue while he was strangling her. After the scare, he kissed her cheeks & apologized. He was afraid that she would outlive him & he hasn't found a cure or means to shorten her. Not too short. Strangling is too short. The clouds are moving too fast. He kisses her

fiercely near the bus
stop. The bus crosses
the bridge & makes
an abrupt pause. The
clouds migrate too
like birds. They too
get uncomfortable
staying in one
position too long. The
bus crosses the river.
Two shopping carts lie
on their side in the
river. It appears as
if the shopping carts
were running away from
prison. Slipped &
fell flat. The leaves
are shaking their
leaf bracelets back
& forth. The breeze
leaves the corridor
of the bus station &
returns unexpectedly.
The woman tastes salt
& vinegar on her lips.
Autumn finally returns
with the nightgown
of summer in between
her lips. She has
been meaning to suck
it dry. Dry mouth &
lips like sinners.
On the bus, a pair of
earphones snake down a

girl's olive skin. The breeze is conducting a sprinting contest. The wine glass will return to Italy to revisit its homeland. Tomorrow spaghetti will pretend to be Rapunzel & will descend the tall tower. Who distinguishes if red gravy is the witch or the prince? Contact will tell who from whom. The summer arrives too late & summer festivities have begun. The room is asking fate to reimburse its vacant life for a more fulfilling one. The woman says that she gets her shoes in central Jersey. The narrator cannot tell if the man she is speaking to is a gay man or one who carries fetishes in his pocket. The room hasn't had the opportunity to spread eagle.

The room remains unfocused.   As the sun beats down the parallel
                                     thighs.   Polka   dot
                                     pubic hair meets at the
                                     center where the legs
                                     converge. The breeze
                                     passes through. Though
                                     waiting for 92 & the
                                     hill is entertaining
                                     the restaurant. The
                                     sun   unregisters its
                                     name from the wedding
                                     album of the 2nd day
                                     of July. A woman
                                     in pink carrying a
                                     bouquet of bright
                                     flowers sits down on a
                                     stone bench. Another
                                     woman in a blue dress
                                     leans against the bus
                                     pane hiding from the
                                     intensity of the sun.
                                     She is wearing black
                                     tennis shoes & maroon-
                                     colored socks. The sun
                                     is unable to enter the
                                     bus as a passenger so
                                     it rides the bus like
                                     a train hopper, along
                                     the railing. A baby
                                     in a striped jumper
                                     enters the bus with
                                     his cheeks bruised
                                     from kissing the
                                     earth. Purple grapes

& elbows dark & darker
where the sun cannot
touch the darkness.
The remains stay quiet
in the hotel room.
Morning addresses the
gossamer light. The
truck ten feet tall
hums a taco sonata,
beef & guacamole,
crispy lettuce &
beans. On the salsa-
dancing floor, a man
named Nephis Meanders
introduces himself.
His muscles are strong
& lanky. The Belgian
beer can't help itself,
smiling in the mouth
of a thirty year old.

The room is trying hard not to grow flowers from the cement of
its skirt. The
tulips bloom along
the concrete of its
foundation. At night
the room inhales
the scent of the
nightshade family &
develops bronchitis
the following morning.
The scents descend the
slippery slope of the

sidings. Sometimes it's
lung-breaking inhaling
the afternoon.

A dress the size of a football field appears in a man's mouth as
he   dreams   about
swallowing   an
alligator.   In   the
afternoon,   the   dress
in its full regalia,
crawls back into the
river. It lies on the
murky marsh waiting to
open its hemmed jaw,
waiting to stalk its
prey. By one in the
morning,   the   throat
of the dress is filled
with blood, limbs, &
hair. The dress cannot
be worn with milkweed
pretending   to   be
parasites.

The room believes that the medley of aromas of porcupine grass,
sideoats grama, common
evening   primrose,
wild parsnip, prairie
cordgrass, & alumroot
stationed   on   the
long corridor of the
prairie has invaded
the   western   side   of
its dominion. The long

80

stems of the grass
hover on the sill.
There is no point to
being famous. It does
not last. Or to extend
immortality.   For
instance, Robert Frost
is simply another name
for a chair & Emily
Dickinson is also
another name for a
type of prairie grass.
There is no point to
reproduce. This is why
the prairie flowers
keep on reproducing
without thinking about
the human spirit. The
human spirit groans.
The room is dreaming
of the flesh of these
prairie grasses to
bloom right into the
mouth of the house.
The grass is quite
robust.   Sometimes
it has a mouth like
a sword. & when it
enters the stone, it
stops asphyxiating for
florescent light. The
room is veiled by the
long slender frame of
the porcupine grass.

Their rigid leaves arch, trying to occupy every breath of the blue sky. The room is nurturing a silent wound near these prairie seedlings. The afternoon is long. The room is illuminating. The breeze arrives to make the white curtains pregnant. The seeds are dancing, waiting to drop their weight, as if they were out at large, avoiding being captured. Monocarpic & oblong, these grasses distinguish themselves from other creatures that inhabit the vicinity of the room by not ever going away. The room experiences all degrees of verdant companionship. In their adult life, the grasses turn their elliptical knives inward, a way of committing suicide without ever doing it. The room is a euthanasist.

The teapot is having a substance abuse problem. Instead of exhaling steam, it inhales white powder. After the addiction gets worse — instead of inhaling, it stuffs itself with a bellyful of cocaine. In fact, its spout is jammed with so much powder that it feels as if some mechanic has caulked it. Sealed it. The teapot won't enter a prevention program. As the years pass, the content inside of the teapot ebbs & flows. Once it curbed its addiction to below the waist. & one day, the teapot finds itself all alone & its bottom empty. & the teapot begins to journey into sea to fill up its belly again. & when it enters the sea, it falls soon after to the bottom. It dreams of having its stomach pumped & its spout rerouted to a new home, a cardboard box.

The room remembers feeling abnormal. The heart is rising. The long body of light is stretching its legs. Out. From the corner, daylight buries its hands in a dream. The room is suspended with this feeling of euphoria. In entering the realm of happiness, the room feels like a vegetable.

The room tries to recall what it is like to be minimal, single, empty, without longing for antique things, stationary objects like itself. A sofa or hutch or something else. But even inanimate objects move. & the room's mind is suspended in space. To recollect the past the way dust collects itself on bookshelves & bed sheets as the light arrives crawling on its hands & knees. Begging. The chair is floating through the

room when it injures
the edge of the room.
This was a week ago
& the chair hasn't
apologized. It is not
that the chair is not
inclining nor is it
filled with pride. The
room is sensitive & to
apologize would reopen
the wound & ignite
a nostalgic sorrow
incapable of remedy.
The chair remains
silent, passing
through. Passing
through the hallway,
taking furtive glances
at the room. The room
remembers the injury.
Of feeling flesh has
been scraped off. Being
awake.

The room is suffering backache from holding up its spine. The
room decreases its
thought. The room is
suffering. The black
charcoal smoke enters
the room. Enters
through the screen &
through the window.
The room remembers
now, the way the sun

was masturbating on
the front porch & the
sweating front door &
the low deck hiding in
the moisture.

Everywhere the room is bursting into tears. The door, having lost
its heart to the
bookcase, is no longer
facing the south window
near the pantry. The
door has been lifted
up to the attic by
the invisible hands
of the landlord to
make another quarter
for the brothel
girl. Underneath
the structure of the
attic, the door ceases
menstruating.

The emotions are woolgathering on the bed sheets. While the
sheets count their
inner threads, the
reasonable mind
hitchhikes on the puffy
terrain of the pillow.

The room is daydreaming. Its mouth is making circles around the
atmosphere of the
dresser before orbiting

the inverted crater,
the breast. The mouth,
in essence, is orbiting
the breast. It is very
motivating, knowing
there are no gates for
tops & halters.

The room is terrified of the way the birds have been diving
through the air. The
room can't imagine a
life chained to aviary
stones. To fly is to
inevitably be chained
to the air. Without
borders & without
parameters. The room
is never expected
to flap its wings nor
descend the cliffs in
any order.

The room says to another room: I gave a rooster to a friend. He
was too noisy. He keeps
on attacking the girls.
The rolling stone. Is
someone who is not
tied down. A rolling
stone. Does not have
roots. When I met you,
I was a rolling stone.
I like having roots. I
like having a family.
The only thing that

is keeping me from
rolling is resource.
A dirty joke. I got a
sweater for a sweater.
I wanted a moaner. But
I got a sweater. Two
drums fall off a cliff.

The room acknowledges, as it hasn't been able to acknowledge due
to low self esteem...
that it can't fantasize
any more. The room
fantasizes daily about
acquiring & inhabiting
a larger space such as
a ballroom. But if a
room were to become a
ballroom, it would not
be itself any more. It
would lose itself in
fulfilling its fantasy.
Others may think that
in the room becoming
a ballroom, it's
becoming a better,
more fleshed out self.

The room mistakes the sound of the oncoming train for one note of
a piano key dropping
down the well. The
room is baffling with the
concept of sadness.
The room has not

experienced moodiness since last July. Cannot take international phone calls. & cannot subscribe to Vanity nor to Wine Spectator. The melancholic milieu of the wine glass begins to penetrate the room's spirit. The Hendrick's gin in the second cabinet of the hutch is a vacant temptation for the room. A dark, queer impulse begins to fall on the room's temperament. The room feels trapped by the indolence of its mind & the way emotions, like the colostomy bag, fall out of the room's stomach. The source of the room's sadness remains unknown to everyone, including the ceiling fan, which hears & knows everything. The room has a personal helicopter, which does not fly anywhere & parks conspicuously like clouds. The room

is determined to
alter its emotional
state. To become more
visually positive. To
feel less disenchanted
by the vagaries of the
dreamer's footsteps.
The room's mood
swings begin late in
the afternoon, in
segments of time,
collated words, before
it shifts its moods.
The room's emotions
depends on the words
of strangers & it is
largely conditioned
to take compliments
well: this room is
absolutely stunning! I
can't wait to have a
room just like that!

The bed sheet which drags itself out of bed, lifts its corners
before wrapping
itself, the elusive
hole, its soul. The bed
sheet has had terrible
dreams, though not
close to the caliber
of nightmares. The bed
sheet has surrendered

to these lucid dreams,
sometimes   finding
itself   soaked   to
the   thread.   Cotton.
Mirage. Light.

The room watches as the tree branches droop into the periphery.
The   room   wishes   it
could   disappear   into
the   night.   The   room
is   courteous   of   its
environs.   The   room
watches as a young girl
with   a   dolmen   hairdo
cuts across the field.

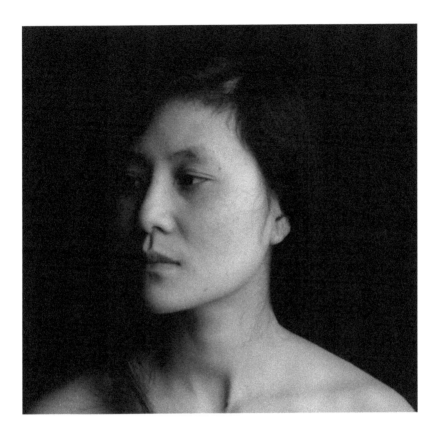

Photo Credit: Scott Indermaur

ABOUT THE AUTHOR

VI KHI NAO is the author of four poetry collections: *Human Tetris* (11:11 Press, 2019) *Sheep Machine* (Black Sun Lit, 2018), *Umbilical Hospital* (Press 1913, 2017), *The Old Philosopher* (winner of the Nightboat Prize for 2014), & of the short stories collection, *A Brief Alphabet of Torture* (winner of the 2016 FC2's Ronald Sukenick Innovative Fiction Prize), the novel, *Fish in Exile* (Coffee House Press, 2016). Her work includes poetry, fiction, film & cross-genre collaboration. She was the Fall 2019 fellow at the Black Mountain Institute: https://www.vikhinao.com

11:11 Press is an American independent literary
publisher based in Minneapolis, MN.
Founded in 2018, 11:11 publishes innovative
literature of all forms and varieties. We believe
in the freedom of artistic expression, the
realization of creative potential, and the
transcendental power of stories.

Printed in the USA
CPSIA information can be obtained
at www.ICGtesting.com
LVHW061111181223
766705LV00057B/3375